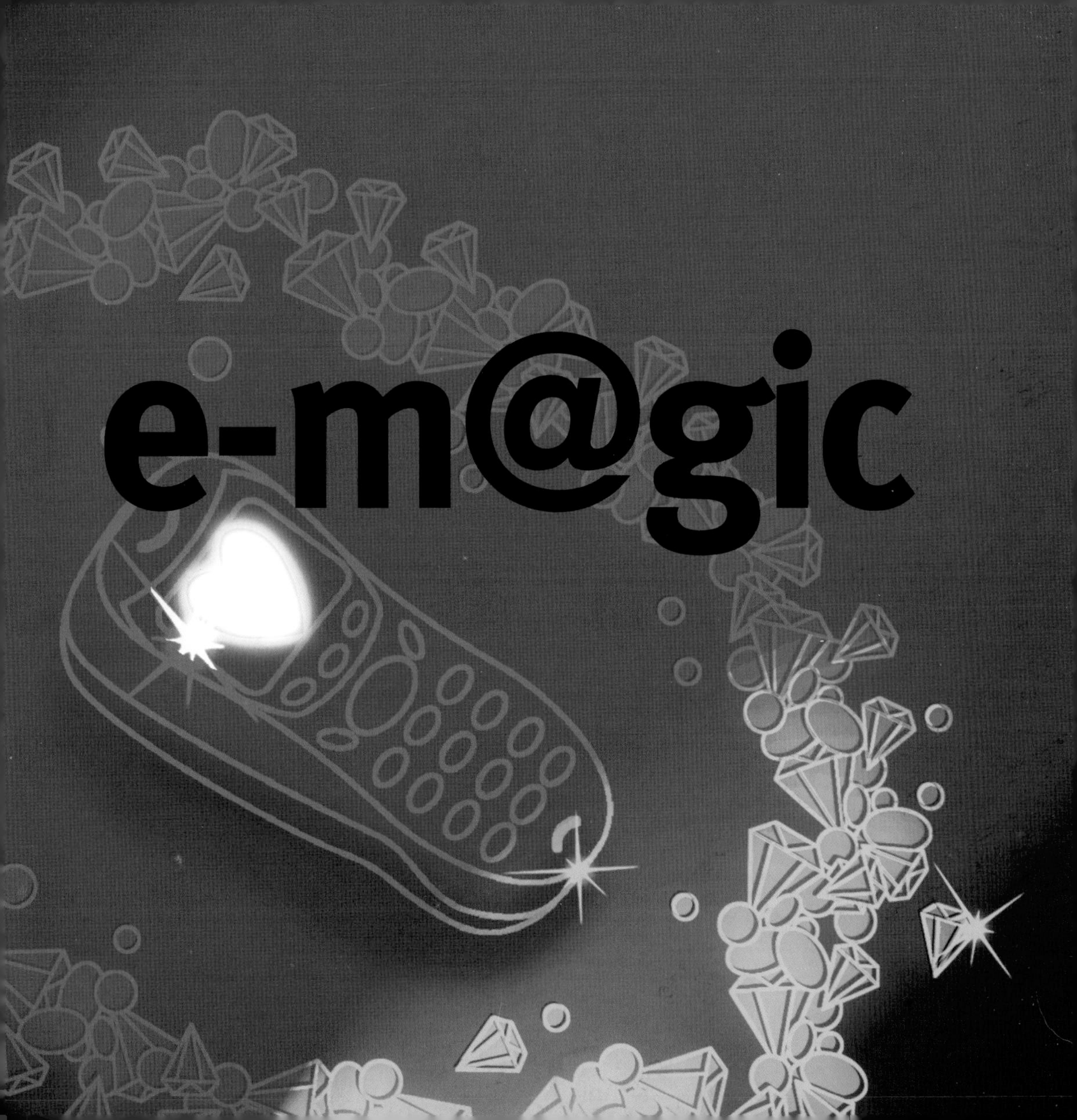
e-m@gic

THIS IS A CARLTON BOOK

Text, design and illustration copyright
© 2001 Carlton Books Limited

This edition published by Carlton Books Limited 2001
20 Mortimer Street, London W1T 3JW

A CIP catalogue record for this book is available from the
British Library

ISBN paperback 1 84222 454 9
ISBN hardback 1 84222 422 0

Printed and bound in Italy

Editorial Manager: Venetia Penfold
Art Director: Penny Stock
Project Editor: Zia Mattocks
Editor: Siobhán O'Connor
Designer: Lucky Huynh
Production Controller: Janette Davis

# e-m@gic

cast 50 spells by e-mail & text message
## amanda craven

CARLTON
BOOKS

# contents

# introduction

Magic is mostly in the mind. You need to believe that it will work, but you also need to calm and relaxed about the results. Think bar of soap in the bath: the harder you grab onto it, the more it slips away from you. Hold it lightly, however, and you have a much better chance of stirring up some suds! So it is with spellmaking. Remain cool and you'll get what you want ... eventually.

A good witch or wizard, however, also knows it's important to persist, up to a point. If things still aren't happening, they have a good think about their motives. Witchcraft, like most things, has its rules. The number one rule is not to hurt anyone or anything else by your actions – and that includes the bitch from hell that stole your boyfriend. Closely following on the heels of this, rule number two states that anything you do will come back on you three times over.

It doesn't take a genius to work out, therefore, that opting for good works better every time, if only for your own sake. Basically, do unto others only what you would do to your precious little self and life will stay sweet. Give in to that temptation to wish a thousand evil thoughts on someone and you only have yourself to blame when it all goes pear-shaped.

All the spells in this book are easy to perform and a lot of them make use of the sort of technical toys we use each and every day, especially that most essential life accessory, the mobile (cell) phone. Texting is great for magic making, being fast, effective and, above all, fun. Magic is more about play than work; the more fun you have doing it, the better. A successful witch is one who's having a blast.

You will notice that a lot of the spells use similar ingredients. This helps to keep things both simple and cheap. You can find all the ingredients easily enough in local shops, and some addresses are given at the back of the book to help even more. You will also find lists of m@gicons, symbols you can download, colour magical meanings and crystal magical meanings. Use these as a guide, but remember that these are your spells. Never be afraid to adapt or create a spell to suit you. The best magic is always that which we make up ourselves. Have a wicked time spellweaving!

# 1

witching hour

# charge up those chakras

This is a great one to do as your first ever text spell, involving as it does all your chakras, or energy centres. You can perform this when you feel that life is a bit out of control or when all your best efforts seem to be getting you nowhere fast. Charging up your chakras will help you get back on top of things, adding a magical impetus to all that you want to achieve.

## YOU WILL NEED:

••• **mobile (cell) phone**

## Chakra Locations and Meanings

|  | Colour | Location | Simple Meaning |
|---|---|---|---|
| Base chakra | Red | Genital area | Power |
| Sacral chakra | Orange | Just below belly button | Creativity |
| Stomach chakra | Yellow | 7.5 cm (3 in) above belly button | Pleasure, emotion |
| Heart chakra | Green | Within your heart | Love (all types) |
| Throat chakra | Blue | Within your throat | Communication |
| Third eye chakra | Indigo | Centre of forehead | Psychic ability |
| Crown chakra | Violet | Top of head | Spiritual connection |

*The first part of this spell is crucial, so take the time to get it right. Make sure you read through the instructions completely before you even begin.*

**1** Sit calmly and quietly in a comfortable position and close your eyes. Silently count down from ten to one, concentrating only on the numbers. If another thought pops into your head, begin again. This may seem a bit tough, but it's important that you clear your mind totally. Thinking only of the numbers will help you to reach that magically meditative state.

**2** When you have successfully counted down from ten, try to sit for a moment with a mind full of nothing. It may sound weird, but if you try it you'll know what I mean. If this really is an impossible task, imagine that your mind is full of deep, still water or soft, black velvet. These two images often help when first learning to let go and sink into nothingness – an important skill to learn if you are going to perform really powerful magic. All the best spells are cast when our minds are free of clutter and distraction; master this art and you will become one of the best spellcasters around.

**3** The blank mind bit need only last for a minute or two at first. Any longer and stray thoughts will inevitably drift in to confuse the issue. You now need to begin to charge up your chakras. Begin by imagining that you are sitting on the burning embers of a fire. See those embers as glowing a deep red, the colour of the base chakra. Start to see flames licking up from the embers, flickering first as orange into your belly and then growing higher, reaching up to your waist with yellow tips. The flames reach higher, touching your heart area with green and then lighting up your throat with a bright blue. Now indigo or deep purple in colour, they reach the space on your forehead between your eyes, your third eye. Finally, flickering on up from the third eye, they touch the area above the crown of your head, ending in a violet haze.

**4** Really visualize the flames reaching up through those centres, filling you with all the magical energy that you need. When you feel really energized and powerful, open your eyes and tap this out as a message on your mobile (cell) phone:

>> **7 6 5 4 3 2 1**

As you hit each key, mentally work back down the chakras so that the number seven is violet, six indigo, five blue and so on. Hold the phone and imagine it almost buzzing with the energy of the colours and the chakras which they represent. Now send the message to yourself. When it arrives, imagine yourself glowing even brighter with each colour in turn. The more you practise this ritual, the better the results. Incorporate it into your routine on a weekly basis for an amazing difference to your life and your witchy workings.

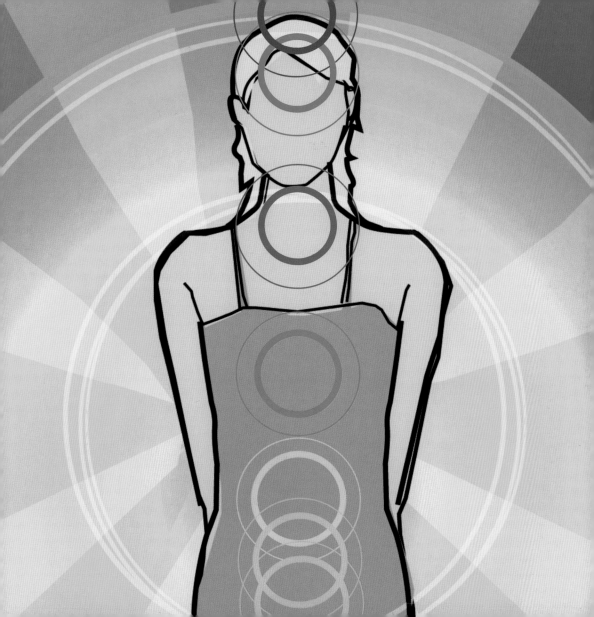

# reuuing-up
# ritual

**Before you even begin to make magic, you should perform this ritual to get you ready to give it your all as an ultra-modern witch. Repeat it any time you have an important spell to perform – do the mini-version if you don't have time for the full shebang.**

**1** First of all, stand in the centre of your quiet space and relax. Close your eyes and imagine the room filling with white light, a light that surrounds you and gets brighter and brighter until it's almost blinding. In your mind, form the light into a circle that surrounds you and makes you feel incredibly safe. This imaginary circle stays in place right until the end of your ritual – once it is in place, you can forget about it and just know that it's there, doing its job.

**2** Sit on the floor, keeping your eyes closed if you can, and relax a little more. Breathe slowly and deeply, and let your mind empty as much as possible. Don't get hung up on this – if a thought comes into your head, simply let it go again.

**3** Now begin to imagine a warm shower running over you, a shower made of soft white light. As the shower runs, it washes away any negativity or obstacles, leaving you feeling totally relaxed, but at the same time capable of anything. The shower stops and, just like a cosmic carwash, you are now being toasted by hot rays of golden sunlight. Feel it warm you right from the top of your head all the way through to the ends of your fingers and toes, almost making them tingle. Remember any thoughts or images that come to you at this time – they might be incredibly creative or helpful, or they may mean nothing at all. Treat these thoughts and images as you do dreams, taking note only if they signify something to you.

**4** Focus on the white circle of light that you created earlier and that has been there throughout the ritual. Imagine it shrinking closer and closer to you, until it finally disappears into your skin and rests in your belly as a tiny white light.

**5** Open your eyes slowly and stand up. Have a good stretch and go off and do something you enjoy.

*The mini-version of this ritual is useful when you want to perform an instant spell or can't spare the time or the space. Just imagine the bright white circle around you and shrink to fit. See it surrounding you, as close as you can. Perform the spell and then let the circle of light disappear into your belly. It couldn't be simpler and works when you need a quick fix of cosmic power and protection.*

## YOU WILL NEED:

**••• a quiet space**

# love & lust

2

# you've got mail

**Here's one for when there's not even a sniff of someone around to cuddle up to and you're fed up with forever finding frogs.**

**This is an update on the Love List, a wonderful magical tool for bringing someone or something into your life.**

**1** First, sit down and decide what it is that you are really seeking in a partner. Think carefully about how you want them to look – right down to the colour of their eyes and whether or not they change their socks on a daily basis. What about personality? Do they really need to have one? Age, height, likes, dislikes – all of these can come into play.

**2** When you are as sure as you can ever be that you know what you want, type out a list. It's better to do this in a word processing package first, as you may want to add or detract from the list at some point. You can also add pictures if it helps, using a scanner or graphics you already have loaded. It's important that these pictures depict exactly what you are looking for or you will only confuse the issue and end up with a messy compromise. And no self-respecting witch ever wants to settle for second best.

**3** When you are satisfied with your list, create a new mail message and address it to yourself. Make the subject line really positive, something like 'The person I deserve' or 'Here comes happiness', anything as long as it's upbeat and perhaps even a little cheesy. Here's the important bit: you must put a sell-by date at the bottom of the message, your personal deadline for your love match to appear.

**4** Concentrate hard, believe as strongly as you can and then send the message to yourself. This has a twofold effect. First, you are sending your magic out into the universe so it can begin to work – and where better than cyberspace? Secondly, by both sending and receiving it, you are coming full circle, making the very powerful statement that as you sow so shall you reap. You've planted the seeds, you've asked for what you want. Now leave it up to the universe to bring it to you as cosmically as it can.

## YOU WILL NEED

**••• computer ••• e-mail address for yourself**

# bringing someone closer

**This is for when you want to make them more than just a good friend. Arrange to meet them at 7 pm, to go to the movies or whatever, then do this spell during the afternoon before. If you can, try to do it at around 4 pm, but don't worry too much about the time – it's how much you concentrate that matters!**

**1** Take the apple and, using the knife, carefully carve both your names into it. As you do this, try to picture the two of you together, doing whatever makes you happy.

**2** When you have finished carving both your names, close your eyes and hold the apple in your left hand for a few minutes. Keeping your eyes closed, make that picture of the two of you together even bigger and brighter in your mind. Next, open your eyes and slowly eat the apple, thinking of them all the time.

**3** Now take your mobile (cell) phone and, using your right forefinger, type in this message:

## > *CU @ 7*

**4** Remember, the @ symbol also stands for an apple, an important ingredient in magic spells. The number seven is the number of Venus, planet of love, and the two stars mean that your spell will be protected from any interference. Keep those pictures in your mind as you press the send button; imagine them going out with your message. Consult 'Looking Good' (page 52) to make sure you look totally spellbinding and you're sure to stun them into submission.

## YOU WILL NEED:

••• **apple** ••• **small, sharp knife** ••• **mobile (cell) phone** ••• **their phone number**

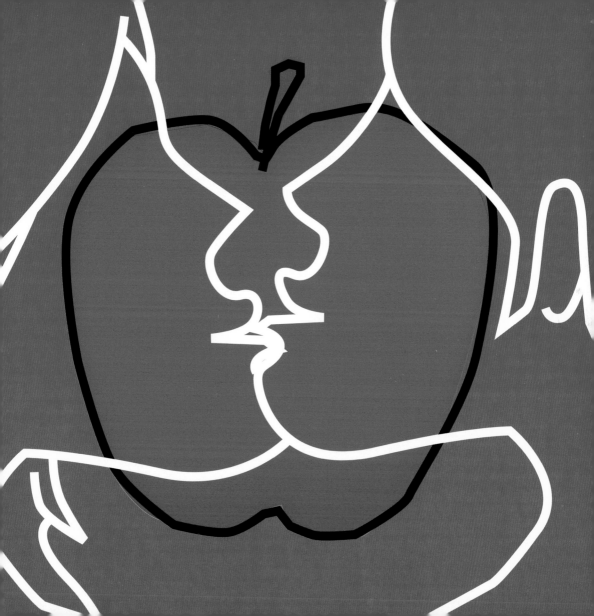

# love text talisman

Talismans have been used for centuries to attract luck and love, or to protect from harm. This one is sacred to Venus, the goddess of love. Try it when the love meter in your life has dipped below zero and you need to generate some heat fast.

| 22 | 47 | 16 | 41 | 10 | 35 | 4 |
|----|----|----|----|----|----|----|
| 5 | 23 | 48 | 17 | 42 | 11 | 29 |
| 30 | 6 | 24 | 49 | 18 | 36 | 12 |
| 13 | 31 | 7 | 25 | 43 | 19 | 37 |
| 38 | 14 | 32 | 1 | 26 | 44 | 20 |
| 21 | 39 | 8 | 33 | 2 | 27 | 45 |
| 46 | 15 | 40 | 9 | 34 | 3 | 28 |

**1** Do this one on a Friday, that being Venus's own special day. Take your mobile (cell) phone (turned off at this point), hold it in both hands and think about love coming into your life in whatever form you would wish. If that form takes the shape of someone fit and famous, that's okay – just don't expect entirely accurate results! You never know, though. A cute lookalike might just turn up and turn all your pals green with envy.

**2** Turn your phone on, almost literally, by beginning your talisman. Select message mode and then tap in the numbers from the grid above, working line by line from left to right and copying the numbers exactly as they appear. Keep to the format shown above, using your space key at the end of the line (but omitting the grid lines!). Most mobile (cell) phone screens are too small to leave spaces between the numbers in each row, so forget those and type like this:

2247164110354 etc. The important thing is that you create the square of the talisman, each side of which contains seven numbers, the number seven being sacred to Venus.

**3** When you have created the talisman, tap in your own mobile (cell) number, take a deep breath and wish out loud for love in your life. Now press the send key and the talisman should almost immediately arrive, bringing with it all the love you could possibly want. Keep it stored on your phone for as long as necessary and repeat as and when you wish.

## YOU WILL NEED:

••• mobile (cell) phone

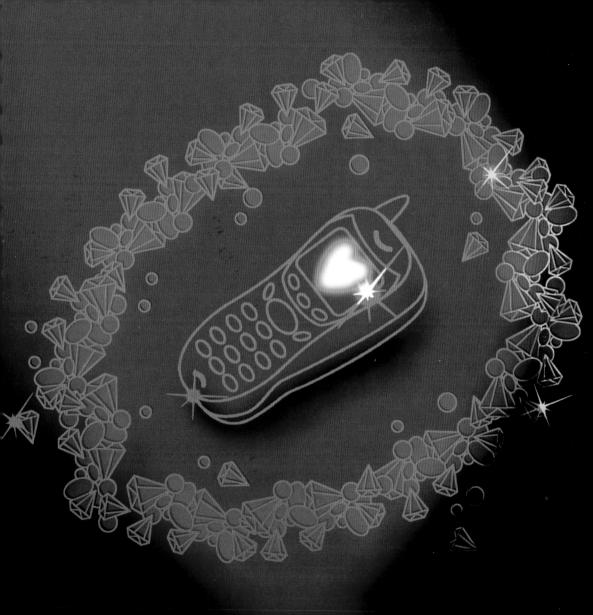

# scan them into your life

**1** For this spell, you need to get artistic. Take each photograph and, before you get near the scanner, practise arranging them together so that you look like one cool 'n' cute couple. You may need to trim them a bit to do this – if you can't bear to take your scissors to that precious snap, you can always scan them in, print out the results and get snipping until you are satisfied.

**2** Once you're happy that you look closerthanthis, make a final scan and print out the result. Put your gorgeous togetherness picture somewhere it won't be disturbed and then put your candle on top, just below your faces. Each evening for at least a week, light your candle for about 30 minutes and meditate on you becoming part of that juicesome twosome you have created in your scan. For even better results, try starting the spell on a Friday close to a new moon.

## YOU WILL NEED:

••• **a photograph of you** ••• **a photograph of your crush object** ••• **scissors** ••• **access to a scanner** ••• **short, thick candle, preferably pink, in a holder**

## YOU WILL NEED:

••• **cherry ice cream** ••• **vanilla ice cream** ••• **cherries (fresh if available, but otherwise canned or frozen, or even cherry topping)**

# cherry ripe and ready

**This is for those times when you need to boost your self-esteem to become confident enough to attract that special someone.**

Cherries are used in magic to inspire confidence, while vanilla is well known to witches as an aphrodisiac – as well as having been proven in scientific studies to turn most men on!

**1** Simply scoop an equal quantity of each flavour of ice cream into a bowl and then adorn with your cherries in whatever form. As you let each yummy mouthful melt in your mouth, imagine the molten ice cream sliding down and around your body, filling you with confidence and making you irresistibly attractive.

**2** When you are finished, set down your spoon, get out there and strut your stuff. You won't want to waste a moment of your magnetic powers of attraction.

# cosmic love text

**This spell is good for those of you who lack confidence, whether it be in attracting that someone special or holding on to the one you've already got.**

> *You can perform this at any time from the new moon up to the full moon, but it is particularly powerful when performed on the night of the full moon itself.*

**1** Relax. Put on clothes in which you feel totally comfortable, play some music you enjoy. If you like incense or oils, burn some that you find soothing and appealing. Create the perfect environment for you, one in which you are happy just to be yourself.

**2** When you're ready, light the pink candle and place it carefully near the window, making sure it can't catch on the curtains or blinds. Take your mobile (cell) phone and, holding it in both hands, close your eyes and ask the universe to give you the perfect love life for you. Witchy wisdom dictates that we should always ask for what is best for us, rather than simply what we desire. This means that the universe then has a chance to bring in someone even more lush if that gorgeous creature you have in mind turns out to be a dead loss. Look on it as a love insurance policy from on high.

**3** Now you need to tap in that magic formula:

## > O*YOUR NAME+YOUR DATE OF BIRTH*O

'O' stands for the moon, mother goddess of marvellous relationships. The stars speak directly to the heavens and your personal information is vital to ensure you get precisely what you ask for.

**4** Before typing in your mobile (cell) phone number and pressing that send button, take the red ribbon and wind it three times around your phone. Carefully avoid the keys or a mixed message might be the unfortunate result. Stand by your candle, hold your phone in your left hand up to the moon and stare at her as you press that button. Ask the moon, either silently or aloud, to bring you the best lover in the world and tell her that you are more than ready to receive. Passionately believe that you are sending your love request directly to that shining orb up in the sky. Say thank you for the love that will come into your life sooner or later.

**5** Remove the red ribbon from your phone and tie it around your left wrist, keeping it there until the moon provides you with a match truly made in heaven.

## YOU WILL NEED:

**••• pink candle ••• mobile (cell) phone ••• length of red ribbon**

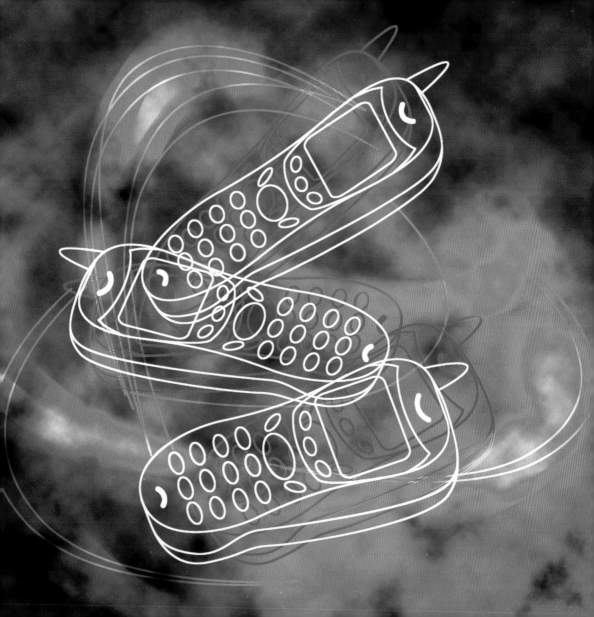

# target them with your text

*Here's what you need to type in to make sure Cupid's arrow does its thing:*

> *Au->NAME<-Au*

**1** Au is the chemical symbol for gold. In witchcraft, only a golden arrow will do when aiming for love. The arrows coming from both sides ensure that love will stay and not merely be a passing fad. If you can, try to perform this spell at a new or full moon, when your target is likely to be more receptive, but don't worry too much about the moon phase on this one.

**2** As always, what counts most is the quality of your intention. Send this message as light-heartedly as you can. Be sincere in your motive and desire, but, once you press that send button, let go and forget about it if you can – otherwise you run the risk of interfering with the spell. By all means, add a message after the initial m@gicon, but keep it on a separate line. It can be about anything – the more casual and innocuous the better.

## YOU WILL NEED

••• **mobile (cell) phone** ••• **that crucial phone number**

Another simple spell for getting someone to notice you. Bells are often used in magic to attract attention, particularly when it comes to matters of the heart.

# ring my bell

**1** All you have to do is download a ring tone that is in some way connected to bells, whether in the title or in the tune itself. Try a search of the ringtone websites and you will soon discover that there are a number from which to choose.

**2** If your phone already has a ring tone that sounds suitably bell-like, by all means go ahead and use it. The point is casually to receive calls whenever your crush object is within orbit. Make sure you keep a check on the quantity, however, or you may find that, rather than getting their attention, you only succeed in getting their goat. If you want to boost your magical workings further, try wearing bracelets, necklaces, anklets or earrings with tiny bells on. Remember the goat thing when it comes to these as well – too many or too often and you could end up reminding them of one of the mountain variety every time you walk past.

## YOU WILL NEED:

••• **mobile (cell) phone**

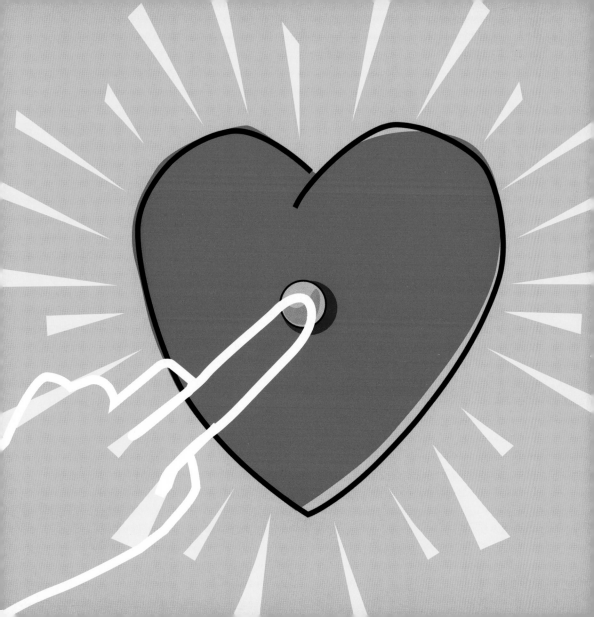

# make them message you

**You can use this to get that significant other to text you, although it obviously helps if you make sure they can get hold of your number! If you have interchangeable phone covers, so much the better, especially if one of them is pink or red.**

**1** Hold your mobile (cell) phone in your left hand and picture your text pal in your mind. Make that crush object as clear and cute as you can and see them sending you that all-important text. Tap in their name so it comes up on screen, and alongside it tap your phone number. Whatever you do, don't press that send button!

**2** Take the red pen and write your crush object's name in the centre of the piece of paper, all the time thinking of that face you fancy so hard it hurts.

**3** Put the piece of paper on a flat surface as close to a window as you can. Place the phone on top, right where you've scrawled those oh-so-sexy words.

**4** Take your rose and clear quartz crystals, again holding them in your left hand. Do the thinking thing all over again, making it even better than before. If you're going to customize, stick the crystals to your phone cover – the clear one in the bottom left corner, the rose one in the top right – before snapping the cover back on. Streak some strong glue around artistically, ready for the next step. Otherwise, just put the crystals down beside the phone, bottom left and top right.

**5** Now take a fistful of sequins and, again, hold them in that left hand. Think hard for the third time, then scatter the sequins all over your phone. If you've used glue, some will stick; if not, leave them sitting on your phone for at least 30 minutes.

**6** This step is extra-special and will send your spell out into the universe. By now, you should be expert at picturing your wannabe text pal. Do it now and make it the best one yet, before carefully lifting that piece of paper up to the open window and blowing those sequins out into the big, wide world. Your hopes and wishes will be carried along with the sequins and, before too long, a text should wing its way to you. If nothing has happened after a week, try the spell again. Sometimes even the best witch has to try two or three times before getting a result. Don't forget to delete everything once you've finished.

## YOU WILL NEED:

••• **mobile (cell) phone** ••• **red pen and piece of paper** ••• **rose quartz crystal** ••• **clear quartz crystal** ••• **strong craft glue** ••• **sequins**

Oranges are often used in love magic. Try this spell when you want to sweeten someone's attitude and make them see you as the juiciest thing around!

# getting juicy

**1** If you can be bothered, buy some lovely, big oranges and squeeze them, thinking lustful thoughts of whomever it is you fancy. You can then sneakily pour the juice into an empty bottle of store-bought orange juice and they will be none the wiser. Alternatively, buy some fresh orange juice, hold the bottle in both hands and think hard of how hot the two of you could be together.

**2** Sweetly offer the object of your fruity thoughts a drink next time you see them. Smile to yourself as they drink your spellbinding efforts unaware, along with the extra vitamin C.

## YOU WILL NEED:

••• **fresh orange juice, either store-bought or homemade**

# get sweeter

**This is another one for sweetening up someone who needs a bit of encouragement.**

Milk is used in magic to make things grow – combine it with chocolate, which is ruled by Mars, the planet of passion, and you're on to a sure-fire winner!

**1** Take the chocolate and carve both your names into it as small as you possibly can using the clean pin. Hold the chocolate in your left hand, close your eyes and picture them treating you as their partner noticing how attractive and special you are.

**2** Do this to as many of the chocolates as you can, then mix them back in with the others in the bag.

**3** Casually offer them the bag and encourage them to take more than one. If they're meant for you, they'll eat one of the prepared chocolates. If they aren't, no harm will be done. If they say they hate chocolate, either repeat another time with any suitable sweet or candy, or, better still, work out whether you want to be with someone who will turn down an offer of chocolate.

## YOU WILL NEED:

••• **milk chocolate (a selection in a bag, rather than a bar)** ••• **clean pin**

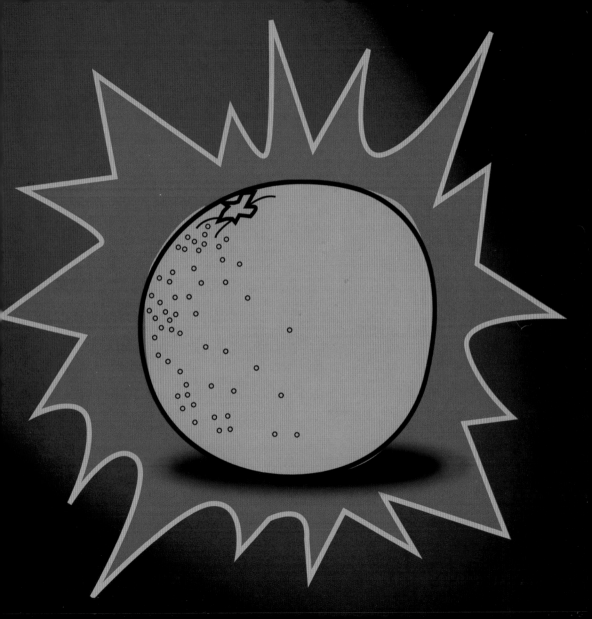

# press those buttons for protection

If you are worried about your loved one, for whatever reason, and want to sleep easy, protect your passion ration by using this powerful spell.

## YOU WILL NEED:

••• white candle ••• mobile (cell) phone

*The more clearly you visualize in this spell, the better the results. Really work at it and the magical payoff will be worth it.*

**1** Sit calmly and quietly in front of the lit candle. The candle is a strong symbol that helps dispel negativity. If you need to perform this spell urgently, however, you can omit it. Most importantly, you need to picture your loved one in as much detail as you can. Make it so realistic that you feel that you could reach out at any moment and touch them.

**2** Now imagine them surrounded by bright white light, shining out like a shield to protect them from all possible harm.

**3** Pick up your mobile (cell) phone and send them the following text, imagining rays of protective white light being sent along with it:

> *** 777 ***

The star acts as a symbol of protection and seven is the number of Venus, goddess of love. You can explain this to them if you wish or merely smile mysteriously, safe in the knowledge that you can relax and let the universe take care of them at all times.

# find out if they are the one

**If you're not sure what they're getting up to when you're not around, and you're not sure what they really feel about you, try performing this magical message spell to bring true feelings to the surface.**

means that the revelations you will receive will also teach you something about yourself. Whichever you choose, remember that ignorance is most certainly not bliss. If they turn out to be true to you, fantastic. If not, the sooner you are clued in, the sooner you can deal with it.

## YOU WILL NEED:

••• **white candle** ••• **knife** ••• **mobile (cell) phone**

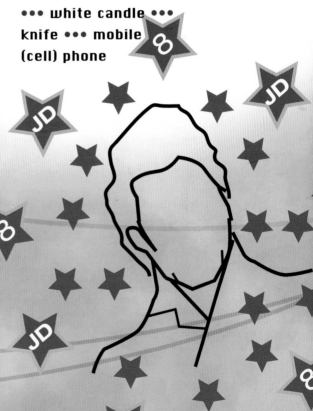

**1** Begin this spell on a Wednesday, sacred to Mercury, planet of perception. Take the candle and carve both of your initials into it. For three nights before you perform this spell, let the candle burn down in equal amounts, until there is about 2.5 cm (1 in) of wax left.

**2** On the fourth night, type this into your mobile (cell) phone:

> *8 THEIR INITIALS
> * 8888 * YOUR
> INITIALS 8 *

The stars help you communicate with the cosmos to find the truth, while the number eight is the number of Mercury, the bringer of knowledge. You can send this one either to them or to yourself. Sending it to them will bring a more direct response; sending it to yourself

# rival
# get rid

Some people just don't understand that thing about three's a crowd. Make sure that rival gets the message by using this simple text spell. Of course, you must make sure that it is in fact the other person and not you who is the interloper, otherwise you could find that this spell backfires spectacularly.

**1** Cast this spell in the three days before the new moon, when it will be especially effective. Black candles are easy to find nowadays and there is nothing scary or evil about them – they are simply used to help drive away negative forces. As long as you are sure that the object of this spell represents a real threat to your relationship, of whatever kind, take both candles and carve the initials of your rival into them, first the black and then the white.

**2** Soften the base of the black candle with a match or lighter and stick it to the plate, just to the left of the centre. Do the same to the white candle, placing it on the right. Now scatter sea salt all around the plate to ensure that your spell remains free from negativity.

**3** Light both candles, first the black and then the white, and allow them to burn down for at least an hour. Now take your mobile (cell) phone and type in the following as a text message:

> 3-<1>=*2*

**4** This message ensures that the interfering third party leaves you alone to become a perfect twosome again. While typing in the message, try not to think badly of the other person in any way, no matter how much you may hate them. Try, instead, to send your rival positive thoughts and wish them well with somebody who is right for them. It is always best to send this message back to yourself as well. For one thing, it lets the universe know that you are to be on the winning side of the equation and, for another, you should remain as detached from your rival as you can – quite literally, in this case.

## YOU WILL NEED:

••• **black candle** ••• **white candle** ••• **small, sharp knife** ••• **sea salt** ••• **an old white plate** ••• **mobile (cell) phone**

Here's a sneaky one for curing someone who is suffering from terminal indifference. To focus their attention back on the fabulous you, get hold of their trainers and literally lace them in tight – provided, of course, that you can stand the smell!

# tame them with their trainers

## YOU WILL NEED:

••• **a pair of their trainers** ••• **a pair of new laces** ••• **two hairs from your head** ••• **a nail file** ••• **needle and thread**

You will have to use your ingenuity on this one, in order to prize their favourite trainers from those sweaty little feet – and it's no good pinching them if they're not of the lace-up variety. Once you have them, however, you can get to work on weaving this very effective spell.

**1** Remove the tired old laces and get hold of the spanking new pair you bought with this purpose in mind. It helps if they are white, but don't get too hung up on colour here – although you must remember to match your thread to the laces or your efforts will be all too visible and the game will be well and truly up.

**2** Sew a hair from your head into each lace as neatly as you can, visualizing as you do so their interest in you growing with each stitch.

**3** Thread the new laces into the trainers, ensuring that the hair and stitches are tucked underneath or through one of the holes so that they cannot be seen. As you thread the laces through, say this quietly, but with meaning:

<< *Now I've threaded these laces through,
So your thoughts are with me and mine with you.* >>

If they're the suspicious type, you may want to grub the laces up a bit, or you can always clean up the entire pair of shoes and claim that you've had a sudden attack of generosity!

**4** This next bit sounds gross, but I assure you it's essential for the success of the spell. Take a nail file and, holding your left hand over the left trainer, use it so that a small amount of nail filings fall into the shoe. Repeat with the right. Shake each trainer in turn so that the filings spread around, saying as you do:

<< *With every step you think of me
Under perfect grace so mote it be!* >>

*This last phrase is often used in Wicca, or positive witchcraft, to ensure that the spell will be done with no harm to anyone concerned – so adhering to one of the basic laws of the craft outlined on page 5. Perform this spell with concentration and good intent, and return the trainers without any awkward questions, and you can guarantee that their thoughts will be with you every time they slip on those rancid rug-huggers.*

# berry the hatchet

**Strawberries can be used in magic to bring you back together with your loved one or even that no-good creep you inexplicably lust after. Just make sure that they're good enough for you or the gods, in their wisdom, may not grant your request. If the latter is the case, at least you will know once and for all that they're not worth it.**

**1** When you weave this spell, it helps to think red, pink and strawberry. Wear something in those colours if you can, particularly when it comes to your underwear. If you have something with a strawberry motif, so much the better. Think pink and red when it comes to your make-up as well, although you might want to go easy on the eyeshadow or you could end up looking more forlorn than foxy. Whatever you do, make sure you slick on that lip gloss (you could also use balm), giving yourself the fruitiest pout ever.

**2** When you look as scrumptious as you possibly can, casually stroll on by and offer them one of your strawberry sweets (candies). If the object of your affections is particularly health-conscious, try offering them a luscious fresh strawberry instead, but be aware this is a little less subtle. If you aren't even speaking, try leaving a sweet where you know they'll find it. Chances are the greedy pig will snaffle it no questions asked.

**3** If they refuse your magnanimous gesture, don't be disheartened. The mere act of offering is magical in itself and will have an effect on your relationship. If they take and eat the sweet, fantastic! Don't blow it by appearing too intense or they'll suspect something is up. Simply smile sweetly and wait for them to make the next move. Chances are that they will, but remember that bit at the beginning about what is and isn't right for you according to fate. Sometimes it's better to get who we need, rather than who we want, and often that isn't who we would like it to be. If you were good together, however, there is no reason why you cannot be again, whether it is as friends or as something more special.

## YOU WILL NEED:

**••• strawberry-flavoured lip gloss ••• strawberry-flavoured sweets (candies)**

# friends & family

# mend a bust-up with your best friend

It may be tough getting hold of a thread or a hair. Think cunning – check out a chair or sofa the person in question has been sitting on or take a good look at something they have borrowed from you. If all else fails, get someone else to give you a hand.

**1** Once you've got a hold of the hair or thread, the rest is simple. Sit down on your own in a quiet place, take up your three ribbons or cords, and begin to plait them together, saying as you do:

<< *As these ribbons/cords*
*I twist and twine*
*So will my best friend*
*again be mine* >>

**2** When you get about halfway along the ribbon or cord, plait the thread or hair in along with the rest and carry on until you get to the end. As you tie one final knot, say your friend's name aloud three times.

**3** Now twist the band you've made three times around your left wrist and tie it tight. Wear it at all times, day and night, and you'll be buddies again before you know it. If nothing has happened after a few days, try giving the bracelet to your friend as a peace offering and let the magic work on them directly.

## YOU WILL NEED:

••• **green ribbon or cord, long enough to go three-and-a-half times around your wrist** ••• **one pink ribbon or cord, as above** ••• **one orange ribbon or cord, as above** ••• **either a thread from your friend's clothing or a hair from their head**

# happy families

**Sometimes our siblings and/or parents simply can't seem to get along, whether with us or with each other. Often problems are made worse if we come from a family complicated by divorce and the presence of step-siblings and assorted extended family members. Try this for those times when you can't stand the tension any longer or when you find yourself constantly turning up the television to drown out the shouting.**

**1** Fill the glass or glass jar with water.

**2** Now take your onion and, holding it in your left hand, mentally ask it to absorb all the negativity and tension in your household. Stick the toothpick through the onion horizontally near the base and then balance the onion so that its base is just in the water and the toothpick is suspending it across the top of the glass or jar.

**3** Take the cloves of garlic and repeat the asking exercise. Bury them in the pot about 2.5 cm (1 in) down, covering them with a layer of earth or compost.

**4** Place both the jar and the flower pot on the windowsill in the kitchen – you can always explain it's a vital biology experiment or your newest hobby if anyone asks. Witches believe that the kitchen is vitally important, representing as it does the heart and hearth of the home. This is why traditionally spells are often performed in the kitchen or using kitchen ingredients and tools, an excellent reason for you to leave your pot and jar there to do their work.

**5** Leave the garlic to grow and the onion to germinate roots that will spread down into the water. The earth you have used in the garlic pot represents the burial of differences, while the water in the glass will help harmony to flow again. Onions are often used in spells to absorb negativity and garlic is a traditional witchy remedy for protection and warding off evil. Give it a few weeks and you should see a great improvement, but make sure you tend your garlic, watering it as and when necessary, and that you keep the water in the glass or jar topped up.

## YOU WILL NEED:

••• **a glass or glass jar** ••• **an onion** ••• **toothpick** ••• **some cloves of garlic** ••• **flower pot filled with earth or compost**

# best friends forever

This spell is especially nice to perform if you and your friend want to bond in a witchy kind of way. Do it on or just before the full moon and somewhere that you have total privacy.

## YOU WILL NEED:

••• **2 pink candles** •••
**old white plate** •••
**pink marshmallows**
••• **skewers or forks**

**1** Before you light the pink candle, you should both engrave on each of them some words that sum up your friendship. These can be as strange or silly as you like, as long as they mean something to both of you.

**2** Light the candles, taking one each. Soften the wax on the bottom of each in a flame, before sticking them right next to each other on the white plate.

**3** Thread the marshmallows onto the skewers or forks, one at a time, and toast them gently above the flames of the candles, swapping over occasionally so that you don't monopolize the same candle. As you munch on the yummy results, talk, laugh and share the joy and fun of your friendship.

**4** When you both feel as if you're suffering from marshmallow overload, let the candles burn down together and allow the molten wax to cool. Once it is cold, break it in half and each of you keep one half somewhere safe. Every so often, you can get together to repeat this spell, perhaps bringing each other a small gift to make it extra special.

# text pal

A quickie text spell for when you need to make it up fast with your best buddy or if you simply want them to know what a fabulous friend they really are.

**1** Simply type in either a rose (@-->---) or a butterfly (@!@) symbol as a message to your friend and then add a friendly few words. As you press the send button, imagine hot, pink light whizzing off with your message. Keep sending positive thoughts throughout the day, adding some more hot, pink light if you wish. Before sunset, you will find that your friendship has either mended or is perhaps stronger than ever.

## YOU WILL NEED:

••• **mobile (cell) phone**

# spellbinding
# success

# lucky break belt

**This is one that is guaranteed to bring you a boost just when you need it the most. Great for exams, interviews or when you just feel the world owes you one, it works best if you do it on a Thursday, when the lucky planet Jupiter is in charge.**

**1** This is a hip and happening way to bring luck into your life using old-fashioned charm and the power of your chakras. Hunt around for charms to do with luck. Good places to look include accessory or jewellery counters, New Age stores and charity outlets. You can also fashion your own charms out of wire, ribbons or even foil, and can pick up all sort of natural objects in places such as your local park. Appropriate shapes, symbols and colours include:

>> *star, sun, acorn, coin, fish, cat, pig, owl, green or red feathers, shell, apple, bell, pentagram, the number four, gold, silver, green, purple, rosemary, bay, small crystals and beads such as aventurine, jade, green agate, carnelian, lapis lazuli*

Try to choose charms that are appropriate for your kind of luck, i.e. for exam success you could choose a tiny owl.

**2** Once you have chosen your charms, take each one in turn and hold it in your left hand, silently asking the universe for whatever it is you need.

**3** Now all you have to do is attach your charms to your belt with your earring hooks, using a skewer or something similar to make holes if necessary. Hang as many as you like, but make sure they're fixed firmly or you could find your luck disappearing down the gutter!

**4** You can also weave coloured ribbons and cords through your belt, twist in sprigs of magical herbs such as rosemary and bay, or add oodles of glitter with glitzy bits, sparkling nail polish and sequins. Generally make it one gorgeous statement to sling round your waist or your hips and receive double benefit from the fact that you've got it lying right by your most creative chakra, or energy centre. Wear your belt or bracelet as often as you can and, if possible, on the big day itself. You will be amazed at the luck that comes flooding into your life.

## YOU WILL NEED:

••• **a selection of charms to hang on the hooks** ••• **earring hooks/old earrings** ••• **a chain or canvas belt (you can find an incredible choice in any accessory store)**

# cappuccino concentration spell

Widely used in witchcraft to attract luck and aid concentration, cinnamon can be added to coffee for a double whammy of good energy and fearsome focus.

*Try to buy your cappuccino in the type of coffee bar where you get to add your own cinnamon. If that's not possible, you can always ask to do it yourself – it pays to be assertive when practising sorcery!*

**1** Simply hold the cup in your left hand and shake cinnamon all over it with your right, sending out the wish for success and/or the ability to knuckle down and work hard at whatever it is you have to do.

**2** Sip the cappuccino and feel that luck and success slipping down your throat. One or two is enough – any more and you'll be the shakiest spellmaker in town.

## YOU WILL NEED:

••• **a cappuccino** ••• **shaker of ground cinnamon**

## YOU WILL NEED:

••• **body lotion** ••• **Hey Look It's Me Potion (see page 63)** ••• **pot of silver or gold glitter/shimmery eyeshadow** ••• **wooden spoon**

# a glittering future

Make like a diva with this spell guaranteed to get you high-beam attention.

Use silver glitter if you want to attract attention of the loving kind, gold if it's success or prizes you're after.

**1** Add a good pinch of glitter or eyeshadow to a small cupful of body lotion to which you have added a few drops of Hey Look It's Me Potion. Blend well with the wooden spoon, a tool witches have long used as a 'magic wand'. As you stir, picture the result you intend to gain by sparkling with the best of them.

**2** Spread the lotion all over yourself, or at least the bits that are going to be on display. Add some matching gold or silver jewellery, your flashiest, most fabulous outfit and a smile that will outshine even your shimmering skin and you're sure to knock 'em dead.

# crystal concentration spell

Here's another one you can do prior to an exam or other big task that requires extra mind power.

**1** Cut the lemon in two and rub each half lightly on both candles.

**2** Light one candle and gently melt the bottom of the other in its flame so that it will stick to the plate. Repeat the process with the other candle and stick it on the plate about 5 cm (2 in) from the first.

**3** Take your sea salt and, holding it in your left hand, scatter it around the edge of the plate and in between the two candles, so that any negativity or interference with your concentration will be repelled.

**4** Put the citrine crystal on one used half of the lemon and place the other half on top, holding it tightly in both hands so that the citrine cannot slip out.

**5** Close your eyes and clear your mind as best you can, imagining a stream of golden light filling it so that all confusing thoughts empty away, leaving your mind as sharp and clear as the juice of a lemon.

**6** Open your eyes, remove the citrine from the lemon and place it on the plate between the two candles.

**7** Sit down near the candles and crystal, and begin your revision or other task. Blow the candles out when you are done, but relight them each time you begin again and remember to take the crystal with you on the big day and at any other time you need its help.

## YOU WILL NEED:

••• **a lemon** ••• **2 yellow candles** ••• **old white plate** ••• **sea salt** ••• **small citrine crystal**

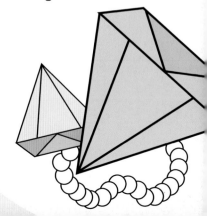

# sunflower spell for luck

**The sun's energy is used in magic to add both luck and success to whatever it is you are trying to create in your life. Try this spell when you need a general boost or just when life seems desperately dull.**

*Start this one on a Thursday, the day that is ruled by Jupiter, and try to ensure that the moon is either new or waxing. If you share a room, make sure you are going to be left alone for at least half an hour.*

**1** Place a sunflower, in its container, in each corner of your bedroom. Plastic sunflowers are fine, as

the symbolism is what matters and they obviously last far longer than cut flowers. If you really want fresh ones, go right ahead and get some. Just remember to keep their water topped up and replace them if they wilt – a droopy flower is not a very good omen.

**2** Place a candle alongside each sunflower, having rubbed each one first with a little of the essential oil or juice. If you are using essential oil, make sure you wash your hands straight away as it can irritate the skin; if you have sensitive skin, stick to the juice. It's the symbolic value of what you are using that matters, so either is good, although purists might disagree. If you do use the juice on your candles, reserve a little for use later in the spell.

**3** Starting with the candle nearest the door, go round and light each one in turn. Move clockwise around the room so that you create a circle of energy.

**4** Sit roughly in the centre of your room, take a sip of your orange juice and make a silent toast to the

sun. As the juice trickles down your throat, imagine it as warm rays of sunlight filling your body with delicious heat. Don't get too carried away or you could find yourself getting hot and heavy with a glass of OJ. A mental trip to last summer's sunny beach should do the trick — the cute waiter is an optional extra.

**5** As soon as you're feeling fabulously full of the joys of summer, spread the sunshine around your room. Imagine rays of sunlight shooting out from the candles, filling your space with a golden glow and your life with resounding success.

**6** When you are satisfied that this is as tropically fantastic as it will ever get, pick up your sunflower ornament and either fix it into your hair or place it wherever appropriate.

**7** Go round your room and extinguish your candles, starting with the last one you lit and working anticlockwise. Wear your sunflower ornament whenever

you can and periodically perform the same candle sequence again to recharge all that positive energy you are now attracting into your life.

## YOU WILL NEED:

••• **4 sunflowers, whether real or plastic (the number four is sacred to Jupiter, planet of luck)** •••
**4 green vases or containers**
••• **4 green candles in holders**
••• **orange essential oil or orange juice** ••• **a sunflower hair ornament or another adornment with a sunflower motif**

5

material girl

# fish fillip

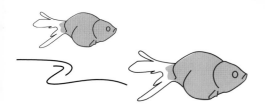

In feng shui, the Chinese art of arranging a space, goldfish are considered to be one of the great 'cures', to be used when you need to boost wealth, in particular. In other traditions, they have been considered a talisman for prosperity and success since ancient times. This updated take on the idea works not only for those of you who could do with a bit more money in your pocket, but also those who need help with study and/or work.

**1** All you have to do is download a goldfish screen-saver. It sounds impossibly simple, but, believe me, some of the simplest magical workings are the best. Let your goldfish swim around in the background as you get on with your life and, slowly but surely, the necessary luck and loot will come your way. If you place a small bowl of salted water containing a few shells and crystals (carnelian, jade agate and clear quartz are good) near your screen, so much the better; a small, leafy green plant will help even further. The idea is that, symbolically, you get things flowing again in your life and work. An added bonus is the feeling of peace and calm you get from gazing at those goldfish all day long ...

## YOU WILL NEED:

●●● **computer with access to the Internet**

# message in some money

You should use this spell when you need a specific amount of money. Remember, though, to ask only for the necessary sum and nothing more. Greed is not good when it comes to spellcasting!

## YOU WILL NEED:

### ••• mobile (cell) phone

> *Before you even begin this spell, work out how much you are asking for and why. It's best to perform this at or near a new moon and certainly before the moon is full.*

**1** Sit quietly and comfortably, holding your phone in both hands, with your eyes closed.

**2** Focus on the amount of money you need and then picture a blank white screen in your mind. On this screen, imagine writing in bold green letters the sum required. Picture it really clearly and make it as big and bright as you possibly can.

**3** When the figures you have visualized are practically bursting through your brain, open your eyes and tap the same amount into your phone as a message. Set it up to send to yourself and, as you do so, imagine a bright green light shooting off with your message.

**4** When the message arrives, read it and give silent thanks that you are the lucky recipient of exactly what you need. As long as you are properly grateful and truly believe that the money is now yours, it should soon follow in a more material way.

# 6

**looking good**

# zap those zits

An old gypsy spell that will help you
pulverize your pimples in next to no time.

## YOU WILL NEED:

••• **a dandelion**

*This spell is best performed in spring and
summer, when the juice of the dandelion
is at its freshest and most potent.*

**1** Simply snap the stem of a dandelion and squeeze
out some of the white juice that appears. Apply
this to the offending spot, saying as you do:

<< *As I apply this*
*milky sap*
*So this spot*
*I now do zap!* >>

**2** Allow the juice to dry and repeat this as often
as you can. The spot will soon disappear, leaving
your skin as dewy fresh as the helpful little dandelion.

# berry berry beautiful

**1** Mash the strawberries with the yogurt in a clean bowl, saying as you do:

> « As I mash and mix
> and turn you to mush
> So you will make
> me totally lush »

It may be stating the obvious, but don't do this part of the spell if you know you're allergic to strawberries. Swollen and lumpy is not luscious and this is how your skin might react if it is so inclined. You can always substitute a mask you know is suitable for your skin and go on to perform the rest of the ritual as described. For most of you with young skin, however, the combination of strawberries and yogurt is a great natural face mask, being deeply cleansing and mildly astringent while adding in just the right amount of moisture.

Take a good look at a strawberry. It's ripe, luscious and absolutely irresistible, and is used in magic and folk medicine to give you these same qualities. Follow this brilliantly beautifying ritual and you, too, will be totally tempting.

## YOU WILL NEED:

••• **6 fresh strawberries**
••• **1 small tub thick natural (plain) yogurt** ••• **strawberry bubble bath or bath foam** •••
**2 red candles** ••• **2 pink candles**
••• **your favourite relaxing music**

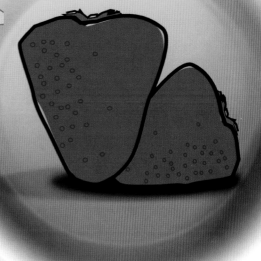

**2** When you have a smooth mixture, take the bowl into the bathroom and prepare for the next part. Place the candles in suitable containers at each corner of the bath or, if that isn't practical, in each corner of the room, alternating red with pink. As you position each candle, carve on it a simple word such as 'irresistible' or 'gorgeous', anything positive, as long as it doesn't make you giggle in disbelief.

**3** Begin to run the bath and add the strawberry bubble bath or foam. Turn on your music, light each candle and dim or turn off the main lights.

**4** Take up your bowl of strawberry and yogurt mash and, standing in front of the mirror, apply it as a face mask, taking care to avoid the eye area. Stand back, admire the result and hop into the bath. You need to lie and soak for at least 10 minutes and, all that time, try to relax and let the mask do its work. Imagine it cleaning your skin of all impurities, making it as soft as silk and you as yummy as its contents. Do the same with the strawberry bubble bath, feeling it softening and beautifying your whole body as you soak. Visualize

both working really deeply, reaching right through to your chakras and beyond (see page 7), making their individual colours shine even more brightly. You can go through each chakra in turn if you like, imagining each intensifying and paying special attention to the red and the orange of the first and second chakras.

**5** When you are done, slowly emerge from the tub, rinse off the mask and pat yourself dry. Apply whatever lotions and potions you like and take a good, long look in the mirror. You will be glowing with an unearthly gorgeousness. Enjoy its effects!

# get ahead of the game

You will probably have noticed that hair plays a special part in magic, often forming an important ingredient in spells and acting as the wily witch's crowing glory. The power represented by hair has been recognized since biblical times. Unleash that power for yourself and you really can get ahead!

## YOU WILL NEED:

**••• rosemary, fresh or dried**
**••• boiling water ••• lavender**
**essential oil ••• a fresh or**
**artificial flower for your hair,**
**chosen from the table opposite**

**1** Put a generous handful of rosemary into a cup or bowl, pour boiling water over it and let it cool. Meanwhile, stand in front of a mirror, rub a few drops of lavender oil between your fingers and massage your scalp. As you do so, chant the following words:

>> *Long and strong you will grow*
*Fast and thick over my shoulders*
*you flow* >>

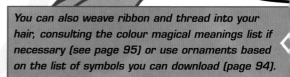

*You can also weave ribbon and thread into your hair, consulting the colour magical meanings list if necessary (see page 95) or use ornaments based on the list of symbols you can download (page 94).*

**2** Wash your hair as usual and use the rosemary tonic as the final rinse, rubbing it in well to maximize its effect. Then dry and style your hair.

**3** Hold your chosen flower(s) or ornament(s) in both hands and ask the universe to help it bring you whatever you desire. It's best to keep things simple by pursuing one magical wish at a time, but you can certainly combine elements for maximum effect.

**4** Arrange it in your hair as attractively as you can and wear it whenever appropriate, making sure you recharge it now and again to keep its power tuned to the max. If you have used fresh flowers, remember to replace them as soon as they wilt. Dead blooms carry an entirely different magical meaning!

| Flower | Meaning | Flower | Meaning |
|---|---|---|---|
| Buttercup | Riches | Gardenia | You're lovely, secret love |
| Camellia (blue) | There's a flame in my heart for you | Heather (white) | Wishes will come true |
| | | Iris | Faith, hope, friendship |
| Camellia (pink) | Longing for you | Ivy | Friendship, fidelity, affection |
| Camellia (white) | You're adorable | | |
| Carnation (pink) | I'll never forget you | Lily (tiger) | Prosperity |
| Carnation (red) | My heart aches for you, admiration | Mistletoe | Kiss me! (also a magical plant) |
| Carnation (solid colour) | Yes | Orchid | Love, beauty, thoughtfulness |
| Carnation (striped) | No | | |
| Chrysanthemum | Wonderful friendship, cheerfulness | Poppy (red) | Pleasure |
| | | Poppy (yellow) | Wealth, success |
| Daffodil | The sun always shines when I'm with you, respect | Rose (red) | I love you, love, passion |
| Daisy | Loyal love, loyalty in general | Rose (pink) | Perfect happiness |
| | | Rose (red & white together) | Unity |
| Dandelion | Faithfulness, happiness | | |
| Forget-me-not | True love, memories | Rose (white) | I deserve you, secrets |

# raring to go with rosemary

**A ritual for those times when you're frazzled from dealing with everyday life and you need to escape for a restorative soak.**

**1** Commandeer the bathroom for at least 30 minutes and get ready to revitalize. Lay out your towel close to hand, then place the candle beside the bath. You can use more than one candle if you wish – just make sure they aren't clustered too close to the bath or you may find things a little too hot for comfort. Don't light the candle(s) until you have finished running your bath, which you should begin to do now.

**2** As the bath runs, throw in a handful of sea salt to purify and help remove obstacles and a small pinch of peppercorns to energize and enliven. You may like to hold the salt in your hand first, close your eyes and imagine any particular problem or obstacle being drawn into the salt, to be melted away when it hits the water.

**3** Add the rosemary and thyme, both of which are excellent tonics which also act as stimulants. Use a good pinch if using dried herbs, a stalk or two if fresh. You can also use the essential oils of each, in which case they should be well diluted in a base oil such as wheatgerm, with a ratio of 4 drops of each oil to about 2 tablespoons base oil.

**4** Once the bath is filled, swirl the water around with your left hand to mix the ingredients of your ritual and to release their properties into the water.

**5** Light the candle(s) and step into the bath. Lie back, close your eyes, relax and let the water take away your tiredness. Breathe in the scent of the water and herbs; imagine every ache and worry being washed away. Feel the bath imbuing you with its magical properties, giving you more energy and spark than ever before.

**6** When you are ready, open your eyes and gaze at the candle(s). Red is the colour of Mars, planet of energy. It is also the colour of the base chakra (see page 7), the seat of our power. Feel the candle warming and invigorating you, feeding you with its light. Do this for as long as you want, then simply get out of your bath, wrap yourself in your red towel to bind in all that newfound bounce and vigour, and quietly blow out your candle(s). Repeat whenever you feel the need, adding other elements such as music or additional scents.

## YOU WILL NEED:

••• **red towel** ••• **red candle(s)**
••• **sea salt** ••• **black peppercorns**
••• **fresh or dried rosemary** •••
**fresh or dried thyme** •••
**rosemary essential oil** •••
**thyme essential oil**

# move over movie star spell

**This is a great ritual to perform when you feel as if you've had a charisma bypass.**

**1** Begin this spell on the day of the new moon. Pin up a picture of whomever you have chosen and place the red candle in a holder in front of it. Each evening for the next 13 nights, light your red candle, sit comfortably in front of the picture and gaze at it. Don't stare too hard or you'll go cross-eyed, which is never a good look, but simply look and try to absorb whatever quality it is about the person you find attractive. Imagine their star quality literally sinking into your skin, giving you that same million-dollar glow.

**2** Do this for about 30 minutes each time, then blow out the candle and do something else entirely. Play some music, go out, watch television, whatever; it's important that you don't get hung up on this, but let it happen naturally.

**3** On the fourteenth night, the night of the full moon, prepare for the spell as you would for a hot date. Put on your favourite outfit, slap on some make-up, spray on a scintillating scent. Sit down, light your

candle and look on the person in the picture as an equal. Realize that you are just as stunning as they are, that you are every bit as magnetic.

**4** Let the candle burn down safely and, as you blow out the final bit of flame, always remember to give thanks to the universe for making you such a fabulous creature. Take that sense of self-appreciation with you wherever you go and you'll find that the rest of the world will respond in kind.

## YOU WILL NEED:

••• **a picture of someone you consider too gorgeous for words, of the same sex as you**
••• **a long red candle**

# hey, look it's me potion

Sometimes we need to remind someone of our presence, to make sure that they understand how special we are. This can easily be achieved by making up your own magical scent, one that you can daub wherever you like to make them remember you even when you're not there.

*This list of ingredients may sound complicated, but the cardamom and cinnamon can easily be found in the spice section at the supermarket (check out the spice rack at home first) and the oils at your local chemist or pharmacy. When choosing essential oils, go with your instincts, but keep in mind their magical meanings as well.*

**1** Assemble all the ingredients, apart from the hair, then hold each one in turn. Make sure that you give each one enough time that a bit of 'you-ness' is absorbed into all the objects.

**2** Pour a little of the almond oil out of its bottle to make room and then drop in the cinnamon stick, cardamom pod and rose petals. Add up to 6 drops in total of the oil(s) you have chosen and screw the lid of the bottle on tight before shaking it

well. Open it up again and, taking the hair from your head, add it to the mixture, saying as you do so:

<< *As I add this part*
*of me*
*So your thoughts*
*of me will be* >>

**3** Screw on the lid and shake well. Leave the potion to sit for at least 3 days before applying it anywhere and everywhere your target may come into contact with it - their mobile (cell) phone, jacket, computer, wherever. Be subtle in spreading your scent and you should soon find they come sniffing after you in a very big way.

## YOU WILL NEED:

••• **your favourite essential oil(s) (see the list at the beginning of the book for suggestions if you need to and don't use more than two)** ••• **small bottle of sweet almond oil** ••• **1 cinnamon stick or a pinch of ground cinnamon** ••• **1 cardamom pod** ••• **petals from a red rose, fresh or dried** ••• **a hair from your head**

# text away that extra weight

Every size and shape is considered essentially gorgeous in Wicca, but, if you really feel that you could do with losing a little weight, enlist the help of a good friend and get messaging to a thinner you.

*First, make a pact with a friend that you will lose a certain amount of weight. It's even better if you both want to trim an inch or two, as you can support each other by performing the spell simultaneously.*

**1** Light the pink candle and hold the rose quartz in your left hand. Think about how much you like yourself and how healthy eating can only mean a fitter and happier you.

**2** Pick up your phone and type a message to your friend, stating how much weight you intend to lose. If performing the spell alone, type the message to yourself.

**3** Holding the rose quartz in your left hand, press the send button with your right index finger. As the message is sent, visualize that extra weight whizzing off with it into the universe.

**4** Always carry the rose quartz with you and touch it whenever you feel the urge to indulge. You should soon be seeing a new, slimline you, one with stellar self-confidence to match your magnificence.

## YOU WILL NEED:

••• pink candle ••• rose quartz ••• mobile (cell) phone

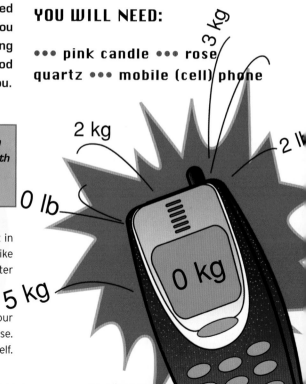

You need to perform this during a waning moon, working on the principle that, as the moon gets thinner, you will follow suit.

# 7

# miscellaneous

Sometimes you may feel as if someone in particular is against you or wishes you ill. This spell will act as a talisman against harm and negativity, protecting you from the bad energy of others.

## YOU WILL NEED:

●●● **clear quartz crystal**
●●● **spring water** ●●● **sea salt** ●●● **mobile (cell) phone**

**1** Soak your quartz crystal in spring water to which you have added a handful of sea salt for 24 hours.

**2** Remove the crystal from the salted water and rinse it under a tap of cold running water, holding it in your left hand as you do so and imagining any negativity in your life flowing away with the water.

**3** Sit quietly, holding the crystal in both hands, and imagine a bright white light shining out of the crystal and surrounding you with its protective rays. If there is someone in particular who is doing you harm, imagine the white light shining on them, fading them away until they disappear into nothing.

**4** Take your mobile (cell) phone and place the crystal on it for a few minutes, all the while still imagining the bright white light surrounding you and

# text un-hex spell

everything around you. Relax and breathe easily. When you feel very calm, take up the phone and tap in the following, copying it exactly:

$$> 4\ 9\ 2$$
$$3\ 5\ 7$$
$$8\ 1\ 6$$

This is the talisman of Saturn, planet of strength, and will protect you against all adversaries.

**5** Leave a space, then add this below:

$$> \quad R\ \Psi$$

The last two symbols are the runes of protection, Reid and Agiz. You should be able to find a similar symbol to Agiz on your keypad, but don't worry if it's not there. Simply type Reid twice instead.

**6** Send the talisman to yourself, imagining beams of bright white light shooting out of your phone as you press the send button and coming back to you as the message arrives. Keep the crystal with you at all times and, every now and then, picture the white light surrounding you, keeping you safe.

# text away an enemy

Sometimes, often for no good reason, a person takes a particular dislike to us or decides to make our lives a misery. If you are being hassled or bullied in any way, or feel that someone is out to get you, perform this blocking spell. Don't be afraid to ask others for help as well. A wise witch is never too proud or too afraid to acknowledge that she can't do it all on her own.

> *Black pepper helps to ward off evil. If you can get hold of some peppercorns and crush them yourself while imagining they represent your enemy getting smaller and smaller, so much the better, but don't overdo the vindictiveness! It's good magic practice to wish no harm to anyone, no matter how much they may have hurt you. Otherwise, the law of threefold return can come into play, meaning that whatever you wish on another person returns to you multiplied by three. That, if nothing else, should keep you in check when a naughty thought enters your head.*

**1** When your pepper is ready, pick up your mobile (cell) phone and enter this message:

> **+<NAME OF YOUR ENEMY>+**

The crosses are a symbol of protection, keeping you safe from any maliciousness, while the sharp brackets act as a magical barrier between you and this person.

**2** Take your pepper and scatter it over the screen of your phone, being careful not to drop it on the keys in case it jams them.

**3** Carefully enter your details to send the message back to yourself, trying not to disturb too much of the pepper. As you press the send key, blow the pepper away as hard as you can. It isn't as easy as it sounds to perform both simultaneously, but do your best. Most importantly, throw all your energy into the blowing, imagining this person being blasted right out of your life by a huge gust of wind. Remember not to get too graphic or mean – mangled limbs and oodles of blood are not what we are aiming for here. Simply see them being blown away, disappearing off into their own little world where they can do as they wish, no longer around to bother you with their presence. It may take one or two repetitions, but you should soon see results with this one and, until then, make sure you that don't suffer in silence!

## YOU WILL NEED:

••• **mobile (cell) phone** ••• **black pepper**

# send PMS packing

**There is nothing like a belly full of cramps and a face full of spots to make you feel at your very worst. This spell will not only quite literally ease the pain, it will also make you feel fabulously desirable even when you are slobbing around in your greyest old knickers and baggiest jeans.**

**1** Make up the following mixture and then stir or shake it thoroughly:

> *4 drops clary sage oil (good for menstrual cramps)*
> *3 drops rose oil (used to boost self-love and esteem)*
> *6 drops lavender oil (a great all-round comforter)*
> *2 tablespoons base oil*

**2** Sit comfortably and quietly. Begin to massage the mixture into your belly with your left hand, imagining it penetrating right through to your very core. Feel it warming and soothing you, bringing you peace and confidence. Keep massaging and begin to picture a flame growing in your belly, starting at the base of your pelvis as a red glow and spreading up in orange flames to reach your belly button as a yellow glow. These colours represent your first three chakras (see page 7) and will energize and give you confidence just when you need it most.

**3** Finish your massage by resting the flat of your hand just below your belly button for a moment and then pick up your rose quartz crystal in the same hand. Enclose it in your fist so that it absorbs the oil that is left on your hand. You can also anoint it with some of the leftover oil if you wish. Carry the rose quartz with you at all times until you feel better and repeat this spell on a monthly basis.

## YOU WILL NEED:

••• **clary sage essential oil**
••• **rose essential oil** ••• **lavender essential oil** ••• **base oil such as sweet almond** ••• **rose quartz crystal**

# a crystal and a cover add magic to your phone

Colour magic can spread to all areas of your life, casting its spell through your choice of clothes, make-up and accessories. Here's an all-purpose spell using your mobile (cell) phone cover that can be adapted to bring you whatever it is you desire.

*You can do this in conjunction with other phone and text spells to reinforce and make the results even more powerful. You could, for example, use a pink or red cover and a rose quartz with the Love Text Talisman (see page 16) and make it happen a lot faster and harder, or a black cover and a clear quartz crystal to add even more oomph to the Text Un-Hex Spell (page 67). Or you can simply do this on its own for a gentle, long-lasting effect that will slowly and surely bring the rewards you are seeking.*

take your crystal out every now and again, and recharge it along with the cover. By being so close to you at all times, the magic has a chance to work in a subtle but constant fashion, particularly when you might be talking to or texting the focus of your spell.

**1** Hold both the cover and the crystal between both hands. Shut your eyes and think hard about what it is you want them to help you achieve. Take your time over this, keeping both items between your hands until you can practically feel them buzzing with your energy and desires.

**2** Slip the crystal into the bottom of the phone cover and insert your phone. If you are going on to practise some more magic, do so now. If not, simply

## YOU WILL NEED:

••• mobile (cell) phone cover in appropriate colour (check out the colour magical meanings on page 95) ••• a tiny crystal, chosen for its properties (turn to the crystal meanings list, also on page 95)

# va va vacuum spell

**Remember the witch's broomstick? One of its uses was to sweep away any psychic obstacles or negativity represented by dirt and dust. Look on your vacuum cleaner as the modern equivalent and practise some good feng shui into the bargain. If you feel that the world is against you or that there are too many hurdles in your path, this is the spell for you.**

**1** Start by clearing away as much clutter as you can, picking those clothes off the floor and cramming stuff away as tidily as you can. This is particularly relevant for your bedroom or whatever constitutes your personal space, but, if you extend it to the rest of the house, I'm sure everyone will be delighted and the extra brownie points you gain will make you instantly feel more loved and appreciated. You could also flick a duster around for added magical impact, moving positive energy in as you send dust flying into the air.

**2** When your space is as tidy as possible, set to work with the vacuum cleaner, visualizing the dust and dirt that is sucked up as the negativity surrounding you. Imagine it disappearing forever into the bowels of the vacuum, leaving your life free of angst or impediment.

**3** Once you are satisfied that the floor is squeaky clean, turn off the vacuum cleaner, sit down in the middle of the room and close your eyes. Imagine yourself filling with bright white light. Open your eyes and send the light out into the room from the space between your eyebrows known as your third, or psychic, eye. Have fun with this – make those rays shoot all round the place, whizzing and whirling as they change the energy in your space into one that is totally positive.

**4** When you are ready, stand up, take your bottle of water, to which you have added about 6 drops of lavender oil, and spritz the room thoroughly, making sure you get into each and every corner. Lavender helps dispel negativity, while water represents a new flow in your affairs. By doing this, you are helping to boost and maintain the effects of your meditation.

**5** Relax and let the beneficial effects flood into your life, repeating the spell whenever necessary. This is also a good one to use if your household seems to be suffering from tension and negativity. If so, you will have to grit your teeth and vacuum and spritz the place from top to bottom. The results will be worth the effort.

## YOU WILL NEED:

••• **vacuum cleaner** ••• **water spray bottle (like the ones used for ironing or gardening)** ••• **lavender essential oil**

# scare away something bad

**Based on an ancient Chinese ritual, this spell comes in handy when you need to get someone or something out of your life.**

**1** Mix a handful of each of the ingredients together in a bowl and stir with a wooden spoon. As you stir, focus on whomever or whatever you want to get rid of and imagine them getting smaller and smaller.

**2** Once you are satisfied with your stirring, take your bowl outside. If it's a windy day, so much the better. Whatever the weather, the important thing is to put some feeling into this, so it's probably better if you don't have that nosy neighbour looking at you sideways while you perform your ritual.

**3** Scoop up a small fistful of your mixture and, turning around slowly in a complete circle, throw it into the air. As you toss, chant the following as loudly or as softly as you wish, but make it meaningful:

> " *To the North, South, East, West you blow*
> *So that out of my life X (insert name of person/thing) will go* "

**4** Repeat until your bowl is completely empty, then take the bowl inside and wash it thoroughly so that no trace of seed or rice remains. Allow the wind and weather to do their work, aiding your magic along until you find either that you're free of whatever it was that was troubling you or that it simply no longer bothers you as much.

## YOU WILL NEED:

**••• birdseed ••• white rice ••• salt ••• wooden spoon ••• bowl**

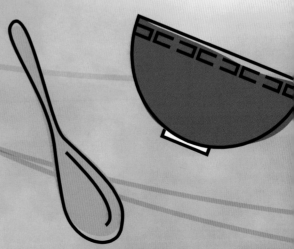

# make it happen with a message

We've all heard that most famous magical word, Abracadabra. How many of us, however, know that it really works and has been used in proper spell making for thousands of years? Use this simple text spell when you have a particular wish or desire and find out for yourself what the ancients have always known ...

*It may seem superfluous to stress this, but it is really important that you know exactly what you want and why you want it. There is an old saying, 'Be careful what you wish for because you might just get it.' It's certainly true that often we don't think things through carefully enough. Getting off with the gorgeous guy, for example, may seem a perfectly respectable desire, but what if he is actually already seeing someone and, in order for you two to get together, something horrible has to happen to that other person? Sure, you might shrug and think so what, but remember one of the basic rules of Wicca – whatever you put out comes back to you three times over. So, even if you have no problem with breaking up someone else's relationship, think about how you would feel if you then, almost inevitably, went on to break up not only with Mr Marvellous, but also with the next two guys you go out with after him ...*

Keeping the warning firmly in mind, it's up to you to work out if you are behaving ethically. Another basic rule is that, when you wish, you will get what you need, rather than what you think you need. Sounds like a cop-out, but if you think about it that actually works out in your favour. Okay, lecture over.

**1** Pick up that trusty phone and type a message to yourself, stating loudly and clearly what it is you want, as precisely as you can. Type this in underneath:

> > *ABRACADABRA*
> > *ABRACADABR*
> > *ABRACADAB*
> > *ABRACADA*
> > *ABRACAD*
> > *ABRACA*
> > *ABRAC*
> > *ABRA*
> > *ABR*
> > *AB*
> > *A*

**2** Take a deep breath, press the send button and wish hard as you exhale. Provided that your intentions were good and you really believed, your wish should come true within the next moon cycle. If nothing happens, perform it again — but examine your motives first. If you're kidding yourself about their purity, perhaps you should think again!

## YOU WILL NEED:

••• **mobile (cell) phone**

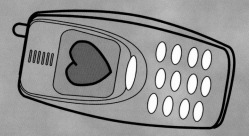

# the t-shirt spell

As you've probably guessed by now, magic relies a lot on symbols and images to make things happen. In this spell you can literally customize your life and make a fab fashion statement into the bargain.

**1** First decide what it is you are casting a spell for and then you can work out which colour will work best, using the meanings list given on page 95. So, if you want to cast a spell for love, pink or red would be appropriate colours; for money or luck, green is a good choice; and so on.

**2** Think of shapes and symbols that would help your spell to work, looking through the suggestions in the book for ideas. A cherry or strawberry, for instance, would be a great choice for romance, an owl an appropriate symbol if you have exams on your mind. As ever, be as creative as you can. Include shapes, words, totems and text in your design. Go wild with your use of colour and shout out loud to the universe, not forgetting the importance of the chakras (see page 7) – for example, green over the heart chakra can only intensify its power. This is your T-shirt and it's up to you to really make it your own. Make sure, however, that you like the result because you're going to be wearing it rather a lot!

**3** Once your masterpiece is finished, leave it to dry for however long it takes and then, the first time you want to wear it, make sure you that have taken a beautifying bath before you even slip it over your head.

It helps if you choose an appropriate occasion – say, the day of a big date or exam – for this important first outing. Visualize strongly what you hope to achieve as you pull on the T-shirt. Wear it with pride, knowing that you are telling the universe exactly what you want for the whole world to see.

## YOU WILL NEED:

••• **plain T-shirt of an appropriate colour** ••• **sequins, transfers, fabric paints, feathers – whatever your imagination requires**

# paint your nails for peace

**There can never be too much peace in the world, whether in your personal space or on Earth in general. Perform this ritual whenever you feel the need to boost that peace factor and send your karma rating soaring towards the sky.**

## YOU WILL NEED:

••• **red, orange, yellow, green, blue and purple or violet nail polish** ••• **white candle** ••• **piece of white paper**

**1** Sit down barefoot in a quiet space to perform this spell, one where you will remain undisturbed. First, light your candle and sit in front of it. Gaze into the flame and calm your mind, consciously letting go of any intrusive thoughts or niggling problems. Just sit and let go until you feel totally centred.

**2** Take your nail polish and, starting with your toes, paint each toe in turn. Begin with the big toe of the left foot and work out, following the sequence of colours given above. Do the right foot as well and try to paint in a meditative fashion, concentrating on nothing more than the swish of the brush and filling in the shape of your toenails. If you like, you can do your hands as well, starting with the thumb and working out. If you are a guy reading this, be brave! Real men can make magic and are never afraid to show their feminine side.

**3** Again, sit quietly while the polish dries and try to make your thoughts as positive as possible. If you have a particular problem, think about it being resolved in one way or another. Send yourself healing energy in the form of white light whizzing around you, imbuing you with its strength and sense of protection and peace. Spare a moment for others in need in the world as well. Send out positive energy to those areas that are hit by war or other crisis, imagining beams of white light reaching out to those who need them the most.

**4** When the polish is dry, take the piece of paper and, using polish, write 'PEACE' in block capitals, one colour for each letter and working in the same sequence, i.e. start with red, then orange and so on.

**5** Fold the paper and tuck it into a pocket or purse, to be carried with you whenever you wish. Blow out your candle, but occasionally remember to relight it and practise the same meditation. This will do wonders not only for you personally, but for all your magical workings, too. If you can persuade friends to perform the same ritual, so much the better. The results will be magnified and everyone will benefit.

# banish that bad habit

All of us have a habit we would love to break, whether it's biting our nails, twiddling our hair or doing something altogether yuckier! Sometimes willpower is not enough and that's where this spell comes in to help you banish that bad habit once and for all.

*You will be performing this spell over three nights during a waning moon. If you can, enlist the help of an understanding friend to whom you can send your text message, someone who will erase the messages as soon as they arrive. It is important that these messages are sent to someone else, as this symbolizes them 'leaving' your life; by erasing them, your friend helps to reinforce the idea.*

**1** Place the three candles on the white plate, then surround them with a circle of sea salt.

**2** Take your phone and type in a message to your friend, outlining the habit you wish to break. You can be cryptic if you like, as long as the message means something to you. Before you send the message, light the orange candle. Orange is the colour of change and will help you get in the right frame of mind.

**3** Sit in front of the candle and meditate on the message you have typed in, imagining the candle is giving you the strength and courage to change. Do this for about 30 minutes and then send the message.

**4** Allow the candle to burn down safely and relax. On the second night, repeat the whole ritual, but this time using the black candle for banishing. Imagine the habit leaving your life now you've set the change in motion. Again, send the same message to your friend.

**5** On the third night, do the entire thing with the white candle, ensuring that there is no negativity so that the habit will not return. Thank your friend for their help and be ready to perform the same service for them once they see how effective this spell really is!

## YOU WILL NEED:

••• **3 small candles, 1 orange, 1 black, 1 white** ••• **old white plate** ••• **sea salt** ••• **mobile (cell) phone**

# protection spell

This is to help protect you when you feel someone is bullying you or otherwise making your life difficult. While it will help to ward off their attentions, it is worth remembering that a wise witch is never too proud to seek help if they find a situation is too much for them. It is best performed in the three days before a new moon, but any time will do if you are really in need.

**1** Take your piece of paper and write out the name of the person who is upsetting you three times. Then write beneath:

<< *As X [write their name here]*
*has behaved towards me*
*So may it return to the*
*power of three* >>

As you read in the Introduction (page 5), witches believe that anything done, for good or evil, comes back to them three times over. Do good and you will reap the rewards; do something bad and you'd better watch out!

**2** Fold the paper over and over again, then take your jar and sprinkle in a thick layer of salt into which you have mixed your herbs. Place the piece of paper on top of this salt mixture and pour in some more until the jar or bottle is almost completely full.

**3** Insert the white candle into the top of the bottle or jar, wedging it into the salt. Light the candle and picture your enemy in your mind. Make the picture really vivid and clear, then imagine it shrinking, getting smaller and smaller until it disappears altogether.

**4** Blow out your candle when it has burned down about a third. Repeat for the next two nights until, on the third, it burns down altogether and the bottle or jar is sealed by wax. Put the bottle or jar somewhere safe and leave it undisturbed. You should soon find yourself left in peace.

## YOU WILL NEED:

••• **blank piece of paper** •••
**black ink pen** ••• **sea salt** •••
**about 2 teaspoons rosemary or**
**basil, fresh or dried** ••• **thick**
**glass bottle or jar** ••• **white**
**candle, if possible one that sits**
**tight in the mouth of the bottle/jar**

# back to school spell

**This spell is equally effective whatever particular form of 'back to' blues you are suffering from. Perform it the night before your return to school/work/college and feel a whole lot better when you wake up to face that first day.**

**1** Pour the spring water into a clean bowl or other container and sprinkle in a pinch of sea salt and 3 drops lavender oil. Stir this mixture with your right index finger clockwise three times, feeling any negative feelings dissolve as you do so. Drop the crystal into the bowl and let it sit there until the next morning.

**2** Next you need to take your grandmother's approach to any problem and brew yourself a cup of tea! Camomile, however, is not just any old tea. As well as being a well-known relaxant, it also helps to keep you focused on the present and gets rid of any past fears or obstacles. So, if that Sunday evening syndrome stems from habit or some past experience, the tea will serve as a powerful aid in promoting a more positive state of mind.

**3** You can, if you like, stir some honey into the tea, as honey has been known to give stamina and strength since ancient times. What is important is that you hold the tea bag in both hands (before you pour boiling water over it!) and send into it every bit of anxiety you are experiencing about the morning after this night before. Next, drop the tea bag into a cup or mug and, as you pour on boiling water, imagine all this stress and tension being dissolved, just as you did in the earlier part of the spell.

**4** Sip your tea slowly and, as it warms you, feel it soothing and sorting you out at one and the same time. When you have finished, go calmly and quietly to bed, keeping that sense of confidence and peace. The next morning, take the crystal out of the bowl and carry it with you all day. Go out and enjoy the best day back you have ever had, knowing that you can easily deal with anything and anyone that comes your way.

## YOU WILL NEED:

••• **spring water** ••• **sea salt** ••• **lavender essential oil** ••• **clear quartz crystal** ••• **camomile tea bag**

# power up
# your bracelet

Many people buy power bracelets, slap them on their wrists and expect them to work. They might, if you're lucky, but there is one sure-fire way of getting them going and that is to power them up. You need to cleanse and charge your power bracelet so that it will pump out its magical effects. This is unsurprising, as most good power bracelets are made of crystals. Avoid the plastic variety, as they won't work half as well, if at all. Power up your bracelet any time after the new moon up until the full moon for high-voltage results.

*Work out what it is you want from your power bracelet and then either use one you already have or buy one that is specifically suitable. Lots of New Age and accessory stores sell them and they are also available on-line. Check out the list of crystal meanings on page 95 to find the stone for you.*

**1** Cleanse your power bracelet by putting it in the bowl of spring water, to which you have added a handful of sea salt. Leave overnight.

**2** Next day, take the bracelet out of the water and rinse it in cold running water. As you do so, think about what you want the bracelet to bring into your life.

**3** Let the bracelet dry naturally. Meanwhile, set up the two candles, sticking them to the white plate by melting the bottom of the candle in a flame and then scattering sea salt in a protective ring around the plate. Stick the white candle to the right of the plate, the black to the left and leave room in between for the bracelet.

**4** Light the candles, if you haven't done so already, and place the bracelet between them. Leave it there with the candles burning for about 30 minutes, making sure that some of the light from the candle flames shines onto the bracelet.

**5** Repeat for the next 3 nights. Your bracelet is now powered up and ready to rock. Slip it on your arm, loop it through your ponytail or even wrap it round your phone and let it do its stuff, cleaning and recharging it every now and again so its battery never runs flat.

## YOU WILL NEED:

**••• crystal power bracelet (see list on page 95 for meanings) ••• bowl of spring water ••• sea salt ••• white candle ••• black candle ••• white plate**

# magical e-mails

**Colour magic is one of the simplest yet most effective forms of spellmaking around. When applied to e-mails, it can achieve a host of magical effects.**

**1** Decide what it is you want and then study the list of colour magical meanings on page 95 to find the one most appropriate for you.

**2** Create an e-mail that reflects one or more of the appropriate colours. The content of the e-mail can be as casual or as meaningful as you like; adding colour will either enhance your message or give your words a whole new meaning. You can also use the stationery option, if you have it, to add backgrounds and pictures that will make sure your message gets through even louder and clearer, even if it's purely on a magical plane. Consult the lists on pages 94-5 or browse through this book for ideas on images to use.

**3** To create an e-mail using images and colour, you need to go into HTML mode. You can do this in Outlook Express by finding the format option and then selecting HTML text. While in the format option, you will also find further stationery options, from which you can select a background and pictures. Be as creative as you like, bearing in mind that it's your spell and the more of your personality you put in, the better.

**4** It's up to you what you put in your message, but think positively as you type it and keep your desired result in mind. If this is a love message, for example, but you want to play it cool, you could write the words in fuschia pink while keeping it short but sweet. Add relevant m@gicons and text totems if you wish, making sure you choose carefully and don't clutter up your message with too many mixed symbols. It needs to be kept clear and simple if you are to get precisely what you ask for. You can also send the e-mail to yourself – for example, you could send a green one stating that you will soon be receiving X amount of money if you are in need of a little (or a lot) extra.

**5** When you are happy with your creation and have addressed it, take a moment to relax and centre yourself before sending the message. Close your eyes and visualize what you hope to achieve by sending this message. Picture the best possible result in your mind, making it as clear and colourful as you can. Now think of the colour that best represents what you want and imagine your index finger filled with that colour. Think positive as the e-mail disappears into cyberspace and then relax and let go, in readiness for a great result.

## YOU WILL NEED:

••• **computer with Internet access and an e-mail account**

m@gicons etc.

| @ | Denotes an apple, sacred to witches | 7654321 | Chakra power | *6(their initials) *6666* (your initials)6* | Find out if they fancy you |
| 7 | Number of Venus, important in love spells | 7i7r7* | Cover-all m@gicon for love & luck | | |
| | | O*INITIALS +DOB*O | Cosmic love attraction | 3-<1>=*2* | Get rid of a rival |
| ***777*** | Lover protection, | | | | |

# animal m@gicons and a few others

As well as the symbols that you can download, here are some that you can make yourself, adding your own personal touch. Of course, they will only last as long as they are on-screen, but they are great if you need a quick fix, need to send them with a message or simply want to add some instant magic to your day. Feel free to invent your own – these are only suggestions and, as you know, the best spell or charm is always the one where you have used your own creativity.

| {i} | Angel for protection and to bring love |
| @PPLE | The sacred fruit of witches and essential in many love spells. You can simply use the @ symbol as shorthand |

| @!@ | Butterfly for rebirth of love, health |
| >^..^< | Cat for luck, creativity |
| Au -> | Cupid's golden arrow (be careful where you aim it!) |
| <)}}}>< | Fish for prosperity |
| 8) | Frog for luck |
| O | Full moon to sustain a relationship |
| (::) | Ladybird for luck |
| ( | New moon for a new relationship |
| ^ oo ^ v | Owl for wisdom |
| :@) | Pig for prosperity |

| = :) | Rabbit, symbol of Venus, planet of love |
| @-->--- | Rose, flower of Venus |
| S' | Seahorse for fortunate messages/results |
| @_ | Snail for endurance and general good luck |
| ~~> | Snake for protection from enemies |
| * * | Stars for protection and direct contact with the universe |
| <=] | Unicorn for protection |

# symbols to download

You can find a great selection of these on tone and logo websites. Either keep them on your mobile (cell) phone for long lasting effect or send them with a specific message for more immediate magic.

| | |
|---|---|
| **Angel(s)** | Bringer(s) of love |
| **Apple** | Sacred to witches, used in many love spells |
| **Arrow** | Cupid |
| **Bee** | For luck in love and work |
| **Butterfly** | For rebirth of love, also good for health |
| **Candle** | Makes love burn |
| **Cat** | Luck, creativity |
| **Dog** | Protection, friendship |
| **Dolphin** | Spiritual connection |
| **Dragon** | Power, wisdom |
| **Fish** | Prosperity, growth |
| **Flower** | Hope, new life |
| **Frog** | Luck |
| **Key** | Fidelity |
| **Ladybird** | Luck, especially in the home. Also good for travel. |
| **Full moon** | Sustains a relationship |
| **New moon** | For a new relationship you wish to grow |
| **Owl** | Wisdom |
| **Pig** | Prosperity |
| **Rabbit** | Symbol of Venus |
| **Rose** | Flower of Venus, symbol of love and passion |
| **Seahorse** | Great good fortune, especially if you are waiting to hear about something (exam results) |
| **Shell** | Symbolizes the beginning of love or foreign love (that holiday affair!) |
| **Snail** | Endurance, general good luck |
| **Snake** | Protection from your enemies |
| **Spider's web** | Very lucky in home and work |
| **Star** | Protection, direct message to the universe |
| **Unicorn** | Protection |

# colour magical meanings

| | |
|---|---|
| Black | Protection from harm, repellent |
| Blue | Creativity, inspiration, loyalty, wisdom |
| Brown | Earth, material things, home |
| Gold | Sun, wealth, success |
| Green | Luck, health, prosperity |
| Orange | Emotion, success, ambition |
| Pink | Romance, friendship, sincerity |
| Purple | Spiritual love or friendship, psychic ability, spiritual/magical power |
| Red | Passion, strength, courage, energy |
| Silver | Moon, feminine, protects against negativity, intuition |
| White | Purity, peace, spiritual protection |
| Yellow | The mind, confidence, optimism, willpower |

# crystal magical meanings

| | |
|---|---|
| Amber | Good luck |
| Amethyst | Brain power |
| Aventurine | Success, creativity |
| Black onyx | Willpower |
| Blue lace agate | Relieves stress |
| Carnelian | Good for PMS |
| Citrine | Wealth, creativity |
| Clear quartz | Focus, transformation, communication |
| Hematite | Antidepression |
| Lapis lazuli | Increases psychic ability |
| Malachite | Healing, intuition |
| Rose quartz | Love, warmth |
| Tiger's eye | Courage, harmony |
| Tourmaline | Healing, balance |
| Turquoise | Health |

# moon meanings

| | |
|---|---|
| New moon | Good for starting something new |
| Full moon | For making something happen/bringing something to fruition |
| Waxing moon | A moon that is growing from new to full – best for bringing something into your life |
| Waning Moon | A moon that is diminishing from full to new – best for getting rid of something from your life |

# useful addresses

**UK**

Mysteries Ltd
9-11 Monmouth Street
London WC2H 9DA
Tel: 020 7240 3688/7836 4679
**Books, incense, candles, crystals, magic tools and ingredients**

Neal's Yard Remedies
31 King Street
Manchester M2 6AA
Tel: 0161 831 7875
www.nealsyardremedies.com
**Essential oils, base oils**

Tisserand Institute Ltd
Newtown Road
Hove, East Sussex BN3 7BA
Tel: 01273 325666
www.tisserand.com
**Essential oils, base oils**

Watkins Ltd
19 and 21 Cecil Court
London WC2N 4EZ
Tel: 020 7836 2182
**Books, crystals, incense, oils**

**USA**

Azure Green
PO Box 48-WEB
Middlefield, MA 01243-0048
Tel: 413 623 2155
www.azuregreen.com
**Books, candles, crystals, oils and metaphysical stuff**

Mystickal Tymes
127 South Main Street
New Hope, PA 18938
Tel: 215 862 5629
www.mystickaltymes.com
**Books, candles, crystals, oils and much more**

Nature's Gift
1040 Cheyenne Blvd
Madison, TN 37115
Tel: 615 612 4270
www.naturesgift.com
**Essential oils**

Points of Light
4358 Stearns Street
Long Beach, CA 90815
Tel: 562 985 3388
www.pointsoflight.com/

Quantum Alchemy
1209 East 9th Avenue
Denver, Colorado 80218
Tel: 1 888 863 0548
or 1 303 863 0548 (local)
www.aromatherapycandles.net/

Rainbow Crystal
Beyond The Rainbow
PO Box 110
Ruby, NY 12475
Tel: 888 480 3529 (toll free)
www.rainbowcrystal.com
**Crystals, oils, books, candles and many other fabulous things**

For ring tones and logos, look in any teen magazine. There are loads of companies from which to choose.

Some tools and ingredients are used again and again in this book. Here are some suggestions as to what to use and how best to find them:
**White plate** – use an old, fireproof white china plate
**Spring water** – can be bought in bottles from any supermarket
**Candles** – readily available in most shopping centres or supermarkets. For more unusual colours, try one of the specialist stores listed here
**Herbs** – available fresh or dried in any good supermarket
**Ribbons/thread** – purchase these from the haberdashery section of larger department stores